The Melancholic Knight

The Melancholic Knight

Seeking Meanings in the Shadows

BRETT R. MANTEUFEL

RESOURCE *Publications* • Eugene, Oregon

THE MELANCHOLIC KNIGHT
Seeking Meanings in the Shadows

Copyright © 2025 Brett R. Manteufel. All rights reserved. Except for brief quotations in critical publications or reviews, no part of this book may be reproduced in any manner without prior written permission from the publisher. Write: Permissions, Wipf and Stock Publishers, 199 W. 8th Ave., Suite 3, Eugene, OR 97401.

Resource Publications
An Imprint of Wipf and Stock Publishers
199 W. 8th Ave., Suite 3
Eugene, OR 97401

www.wipfandstock.com

PAPERBACK ISBN: 979-8-3852-5048-6
HARDCOVER ISBN: 979-8-3852-5049-3
EBOOK ISBN: 979-8-3852-5050-9

05/20/25

To my beloved family: Haily, Oliver, and Greyson,
for the quiet spaces and the unwavering love.

Contents

Preface	ix
Introduction	xi
Chapter 1: The Call to Adventure (Awakening)	1
Don Quixote of the Night	2
Rest in the Rain	3
Lost at Sea	4
The Weight of the World	5
Odysseus Within	6
Mind's Escape	7
The Sparrow and the Man	8
Along Came a Spider	9
Chapter 2: Trials and Temptations (The Path of Trials)	10
The Way of the Warrior Poet	11
A Brush with the Wild	12
The Wildman	13
I, Sir Gawain	14
Ride the Tiger	16
The Wisdom of Bears	18
Resisting the Suburban Mold	19
Wrestling with God	21
A Pilgrim's Progress	23
The Shepherd's Guidance	24
The Bearded Soldier's Bodhi Tree	25
Chapter 3: The Darkest Hour (Into the Abyss)	26
Losing my Temper	27

CONTENTS

The Beast Within	29
The Path to Calvary	31
The Roses Requiem	32
Eternal Recurrence	33
From Darkness to Oneness	34
The Sea of Sagaram	35
The Flower's Ascent	36
Chapter 4: Spiritual Awakening (Transformation)	**37**
The Mystery of Being	38
Whispers of the Sea	39
The Dandelion's Flight	40
Dream of Eden	41
Love's Last Act	42
My Friend the Green Bird	43
The Night of the Vision	44
The Celestial Canvas	45
A Divine Treasure	46
The Shadowbox	47
Beneath the Southern Cross	48
Chapter 5: Return and Integration (The Return)	**49**
Bedtime Love	50
Greyson	51
A Fleeting Joy	52
Carrying the Torch	53
To the Road and Back	55
The Sycamore's Legacy	57
Frontier Sacrifice: a Father's Love	58
The Modern Knight	59
The Beauty of Wandering	60
A Flower Resting in Her Hair	61
Arise, the Ballad of the Last Knight	62
Beyond the Veil	63
The Old Man's Paradise	64

Preface

During quiet moments, and even amidst louder ones, many of these poems seemed to arrive as if from an external source. I would then craft a first draft, followed by extensive revisions until I felt I had fully captured my voice and struck the precise notes.

The melancholic knight emerged as a kind of alter ego, loosely based on myself and my own life experiences. I sought a way to explore intricate emotions, philosophy, faith, isolation, mental well-being, and beauty through the unique lens of poetry. In all my searching, a central question became strikingly clear: how does one transcend and experience the sacred? I believe these poems have guided me on a journey, bringing me closer to that understanding.

This collection represents a deeply personal odyssey. As someone who has always been introspective, I felt a strong desire to explore my inner life through the character of the melancholic knight—part warrior, mystic, and philosopher. Perhaps you, the reader, have traversed a similar path and will find resonance with our hero.

The Melancholic Knight is not a chronicle of despair. Instead, it is an exploration of the strength discovered in vulnerability and the quiet wisdom that can surface when facing our inner shadows. It is an invitation to contemplate the profound within the seemingly small and to find connection in the shared human experience of seeking meaning.

My hope is that within these verses, you will find echoes of your own inner world, a sense of companionship on this journey, and perhaps even a flicker of light in the darkness.

PREFACE

Thank you for embarking on this path with the melancholic knight.

Introduction

From the earliest stirrings of consciousness to the present day, humanity has long sought meaning in a world that often appears indifferent and cold. "The Melancholic Knight" delves into these complex ideas of faith, doubt, meaning, and existence through the introspective gaze of a lone knight. More than a figure confined to medieval lore, our knight transcends earthly realms, venturing into the cosmos to grapple with profound questions of faith and the inherent fragility of the human spirit. Like Kierkegaard's "Knight of Faith," our figure too must make a leap of faith into the mysteries of life.

    This collection of poetry explores the heart of these deep inquiries through the eyes—and the soul of the melancholic knight. He is a warrior weary not only from battles waged on open fields but also from the silent conflicts fought within the chambers of his own mind. He is a mystic, drawn to the whispers of the divine and the yearning for a connection to God. He is a philosopher, wrestling with the fundamental questions that have echoed through the ages.

    Structured in five parts, this book follows a metaphorical hero's journey, mirroring the stages of the melancholic knight's internal quest. Beginning with the "Call to Adventure," where a sense of unease with the past and present prompts a departure from the ordinary, we accompany him through the "Trials and Temptations" that test his resolve and beliefs. We descend with him into "The Darkest Hour," where doubt and despair threaten to consume him, before witnessing a potential "Spiritual Awakening," a moment of transformation and newfound perspective.

INTRODUCTION

Finally, we arrive at "Return and Integration," where the lessons learned, and the insights gained begin to shape his understanding of himself and the world.

Within these poems, you will encounter introspective reflections on solitude and connection, poignant explorations of human longing and the search for solace, and vivid imagery that paints the landscapes of both the external world and the inner self. The poetry seeks not to provide definitive answers but rather to offer a space for contemplation, empathy, and perhaps a shared recognition of life's enduring mysteries.

The Melancholic Knight is an invitation to walk alongside this figure, to witness his struggles and his moments of clarity, and perhaps, in doing so, to illuminate aspects of your own journey through the labyrinth of existence.

Chapter 1

The Call to Adventure (Awakening)

This knight is not a knight in shining armor with a boisterous laughter. He's a man with a soul draped in dark hues, a heart that carries the weight of existential questions. He is the melancholic knight. He had once walked with a sense of purpose, his body strong and his spirits high, but the world had shown him its ugliness—the fleeting nature of glory, the sting of defeat, the gnawing emptiness that even victory could leave behind. This journey began not with a dragon to slay, but with a whisper from the cosmos—a "call to adventure" that echoed the call of his past quests.

THE CALL TO ADVENTURE (AWAKENING)

DON QUIXOTE OF THE NIGHT

Don Quixote of the night,
The wandering hometown knight,
Seeking to fight with the world tonight.
Once a man-at-arms, now a lost soul back home,
Thrust against his will into the ordinary world,
He misses the extraordinary of the war.
Roaming down dark streets lit by neon lights,
In pursuit of a perilous delight,
To fill the void in his broken heart.
He's a feral alley cat, scared and wild,
Often with vices in both hands: smoke and drink.
A Ronin warrior without a master,
He longs for his old corps.
Every mile he drives down long city lanes, he drifts further away,
As if he's going insane.
Every senseless pleasure he chases is just another windmill he foolishly fights,
In a place where he doesn't belong.
He is Don Quixote of the night,
Seeking to take flight into the next life.

THE CALL TO ADVENTURE (AWAKENING)

REST IN THE RAIN

Life has felt like a dying star.
My mind imploding to the final bar.
As if my soul has gone before,
And I'm just a ghost in the machine.

When I'm feeling a sense of dreaded blue,
And I'm barely able to take a breath,
I must go for a rest in the rain.

When I awake in a dreary slump,
And cannot meet my children's eyes,
I shall pray for a dark sky.
I must go for a rest in the rain.

When I labor and bemoan life's demands,
And feel stuck and utterly alone,
I shall keep an open ear to the sky,
And hope to hear the distant crackle up high.
I must go for a rest in the rain

No amount of bottled pills can do the same,
Then to take a long soak out in the rain.
To wash away my misery,
And give aid to live another day.
I must go for a rest in the rain.

THE CALL TO ADVENTURE (AWAKENING)

LOST AT SEA

Nearly four decades alive, and only a few years have brought relief.
I feel like a sailor lost at sea.

So many years are marked by struggle, loneliness, hardship, violence, and destitution.
Always living in the shadow of my elders, never able to find my own sunlight.

Only my duty to my children keeps me here.
I'm lost in a vast ocean, and this ship is taking on too much water.
The bilge can't pump it all.
I wish a wave would take me away,
Either to carry me to land or to swallow me into this stormy sea.

Until then, I shall pray a Hail Mary
And hope a ray of sun shall awaken me,
And a small island can be seen on the horizon—
A place of refuge and new beginnings.

THE CALL TO ADVENTURE (AWAKENING)

THE WEIGHT OF THE WORLD

I no longer have the capacity to be the strong person.
For years I've carried my cross across the dry desert valleys and over the snowy mountain peaks.
But now, with a wounded heart, in my hour of need, I lay alone.
I cannot continue to bear the burden of this life.
The burden is slowly breaking my soul.
Only the Lord sees my struggles, appreciates my labor, and offers me salvation.
I must turn to the Lord,
For only in his warm embrace may I find peace.

THE CALL TO ADVENTURE (AWAKENING)

ODYSSEUS WITHIN

A common occurrence that haunts me of late,
When my heart is about to faint,
I must stop and think
How mental my troubles are.
I must be like the Buddha and take a deep breath.
The Zen Master still chops wood and carries water.
Remember, Marine, you're a member of the proud and the few;
Your trials have rivaled Odysseus,
And your strength is a deep well you'll find inside.

THE CALL TO ADVENTURE (AWAKENING)

MIND'S ESCAPE

I feel like my sanity hangs by a silk thread,
Tethered like an astronaut spinning above the earth.
One false snip, and I'll cut loose
And drift away off into space.

But the best dreams may come by way of insanity—
To peer far into the heavens
And find God on the other end of a great wormhole.
Or maybe I'll come across a great space fleet looking to build a new home far away.

Maybe it's only after losing our mind that our egos can die,
And that we are free to find our true selves.
Maybe we were never meant to be tethered at all.

THE CALL TO ADVENTURE (AWAKENING)

THE SPARROW AND THE MAN

As I sat long faced in my study,
Absorbed in my work,
A little grey sparrow landed in my garden.
He found a delicious mealworm
And then basked in the sun under the tulips.
Now fat and ready, he took a warm wash in the bird bath.

Then the sparrow, done with his tasks, took flight to the sky.
And I, still in my chair, realized I was the captive,
For it was the sparrow who flew free.
A featherless man, I felt saddened by my fate,
Being tied to my chair,
For it was the bird that was without a cage, wild and free.

THE CALL TO ADVENTURE (AWAKENING)

ALONG CAME A SPIDER

Along came a spider,
Full of moxie,
Hiding in a dark corner of the attic.
She has spun a beautiful tapestry of web,
As if it was made of diamond and silk.

But behind the beauty lay a deadly trap;
Few could resist the spider's call
And foolishly fell victim to their deaths.

From the beginning you understood,
But it wasn't you the spider desired,
So you kept your eyes down
And tried not to be bothered.

But the more vast the meals, the larger the spider grew,
Until he was an eight-legged monster
Who came looking for you.

But there was no one left to draw swords with you;
Everyone was either dead or a coward.
And now you wished you'd had courage before
To stand up while you could.
But now your fate is sealed.

Along came a spider.

Chapter 2

Trials and Temptations
(The Path of Trials)

The melancholic knight felt a deep longing to go on a profound, internal quest. He saw the world's fleeting joys as "grasping for the wind," and a yearning for something more real took hold of him. This yearning eventually led him into a period where faith wavered and the abyss of his own doubts seemed insurmountable. Like a hunter lost in a dense wood, he stumbled through landscapes of despair, the weight of his past a heavy burden.

THE WAY OF THE WARRIOR POET

Every day I train in the arts
Like the Samurais of before—
Fully a poet, and fully a warrior.

Reading in the study, so I may gain the wisdom of the old philosophers;
Poetry on the painted porch, so I may be acquainted with the night;
Martial arts in the dojo, so I may walk in peace;
Meditation on the lotus flower, so I may reach nirvana;
Weight lifting in the gym, so I may live well into old age.

There are many paths a person can take,
But this is the path that stirs my soul.
This is the way of the warrior poet.
Watch me grow tall like a sunflower, basking in the sun.

TRIALS AND TEMPTATIONS (THE PATH OF TRIALS)

A BRUSH WITH THE WILD

I once wandered into a wooded willow and whispered wearily,

Doubting if indeed this dastardly danger dwelled in these dark woods.

Quietly I listened and waited, with a timely patrol each hour around camp.

At first—nothing.

Until the unfortunate struck!

Belligerently that brawling bear barreled out of the bush to my bewilderment.

Frightened by my fierce foe, I aimed my rifle's front sight at its brown heart.

Bang, bang, bang!

The grizzly collapsed right outside camp and cried out in death.

I walked over and stood soldierly over the defeated beast—studying its impressive nature.

What massive paws, muscular frame, and wide head it had.

Now that I had completed my job, I began to wonder, like Socrates of the forest, if it were right.

Who am I to call this bear a beast and strike him down?

Despite my deep distress, I decided it was defendable—as I had done my duty by destroying this danger—and I stopped dwelling on my decision.

Ethics take a man far, but fail to defend.

So I traversed back to camp, tending to its tattered tent, then armed with a knife, field-dressed that bear for dinner tonight.

Later that winter, I wore its fur as a hat.

TRIALS AND TEMPTATIONS (THE PATH OF TRIALS)

THE WILDMAN

We're all just guests in the tiger's nest.
We may be safe in our orange chairs of this solarium.
For behind these tall palms prowls the striped beast that mauls.
But the wild man is free to visit thee.
For he has not forgotten his origins.
And his origins have not forgotten thee.

TRIALS AND TEMPTATIONS (THE PATH OF TRIALS)

I, SIR GAWAIN

At the banquet hall,
I do befall
To the challenge laid down by the Green Knight.
Give me the honor
To play for a while,
Before cross and crown and honor.
With a fell of the axe,
I take a severed head
As a treasure from the dead.
But to my surprise,
He rises again,
And I must meet again
In one year's time.

If only I knew,
With the playing of the lute,
How such a challenge
Would take such a while
And forever alter my knightly course.

For it would be him that stirred my soul and transformed me into a Sir.
I was but a boy a year ago,
Focused on drink and misdeeds.
But through the gauntlet,
Found my courage and then honor,

TRIALS AND TEMPTATIONS (THE PATH OF TRIALS)

And found myself, Sir Gawain.

TRIALS AND TEMPTATIONS (THE PATH OF TRIALS)

RIDE THE TIGER

In life, there are treacherous times that test our resolve.
But I have found the best recourse is the Western way of war—
To take a final stand and battle with all your pieces on the table.
Like Leonidas and his battalion of Spartans, who campaigned north to block the great pass,
That's to say, we must ride the tiger.

When the world's on fire,
And everything seems so dire,
You must ride the tiger.

When all is seemingly lost,
And to claw back doesn't seem to be worth the cost,
You must ride the tiger.

When despots emerge from a vile hell,
And you just want to quit and ring the bell,
You must ride the tiger.

When the people all around you have gone mad,
And you're afraid you'll do something bad,
You must ride the tiger.

When you can't muster the strength to render a smile,
And you sit alone in the dark feeling beguiled,
You must ride the tiger.

Trials and Temptations (The Path of Trials)

Either you'll fall off that striped beast
Or tame it with tenacity.
But in either course, you're the stoic archer who let loose the arrow true.
And win or lose, you played with fate,
And you can look back tomorrow and say you played the game with honor.

TRIALS AND TEMPTATIONS (THE PATH OF TRIALS)

THE WISDOM OF BEARS

The hardest type of person to be
Is one too low or too high,
For both are slaves to their condition.

To be the worm crawling through the mud,
Nearly stuck, rarely to see the sun,
And utterly defenseless.

The other is the eagle,
One who has soared so high
That to come back down
Would be a fall from grace—
A height too high to fall from.

It's the bear who is most happy:
Powerful, strong, independent—
A fall feast, a winter sleep,
The freest animal of all.

TRIALS AND TEMPTATIONS (THE PATH OF TRIALS)

RESISTING THE SUBURBAN MOLD

Oh, how I fear that I'll become that dreaded suburban dad,
That man who followed society's plan: who went to school, bought the house, the car, the kids, and the wife;
That man who labors at a soulless job in suit and tie, just to spend his weekends on needless upkeep;
That man whose only reprieve is on the greens.

Oh, how I fear that I'll become that dreaded suburban dad,
That man who once was an athlete but now only watches his kids play sports;
That man who saves away at his 401k, hoping to retire on some sapphire before he expires;
That man who is lonely but never sees his friends again;
That man who is just pretending to be happy but is dying inside.

Oh, how I fear that I'll become that dreaded suburban dad,
The man who was once wild and free and full of dreams;
That man who once stayed up late to watch the sunrise out of the eastern skies;
That man who, when younger, sailed the oceans, saw the jungles of the Philippines, the empire of Dubai, and the hot rocky plains of Africa—but today he can barely afford Disney World.

Oh, how I fear that I'll become that dreaded suburban dad.
I'd rather be poor or dead than become that man.
I shall not let myself become a slave to my trade.
I shall not run on the hedonistic treadmill waiting for my next fix.

TRIALS AND TEMPTATIONS (THE PATH OF TRIALS)

I shall not find my courage at the bottom of a bottle.
I shall love and adore my wife and kids and be a loyal friend.

Oh, how I fear that I'll become that dreaded suburban dad.
I shall not stop wondering and wandering the earth.
I shall not gaze upon the stars and not see their dust inside myself.
I shall not ignore God's breath breathing through the birch forest as I walk down the trail.

Oh, how I fear that I'll become that dreaded suburban dad.
I shall live with virtue and be kind to all I meet, no matter their station in life.
I shall not forget how dangerous I can be as I lift heavy plates above my head, or roll at Jiu-jitsu, or let loose an arrow from a bow.
I shall not stop learning until I'm dead. I'll read the words of the great philosophers and poets and rage with them against the dying of the light.

I shall not become that man.
I shall not wither away like a dying rose.
I shall not die before my time.
I shall become who I'm meant to be.

WRESTLING WITH GOD

I have tried,
As many times as the moon has risen high,
To bow my head and take a leap of faith.
I have wrestled with God.

God and I have loved and fallen out of love, and in love again more times than I care to count,
But the bush fails to fire.
I was not the one who ate the apple red.
I am not the one who raised a sword to Michael.
I am not the one who betrayed Christ when the rooster crowed.
But I am the one who wanders the wilderness.
I have wrestled with God.

I have gone to Rome to seek the Pope.
I have written to the Anglican Archbishop twice.
I have reasoned with Luther the Philosopher.
I have meditated on top of a lotus flower with the Buddha, looking lazy at me.
I have wrestled with God.

Despite my labor, I remain spiritually stagnant.
If only a wise old sage would cross paths with me and explain these mysteries to me.
But despite the plateau, I still get glimpses of the divine:
A bright sun ray passing through the branches of a tree;
A kind stranger who selflessly came to my aid on a stormy day;

TRIALS AND TEMPTATIONS (THE PATH OF TRIALS)

Those little butterfly effects, where small events take flight and fly to great heights.
I have wrestled with God.

Despite my fatigue and heavy heart,
I remain climbing this mountain.
Despite the slow progress, drudgery, and difficult terrain, I climb upward towards heaven.
With a sherpa, or alone, I shall reach the top of this great peak.
I have wrestled with God.

TRIALS AND TEMPTATIONS (THE PATH OF TRIALS)

A PILGRIM'S PROGRESS

A journey starts with a call—
A silent chime only the heart can hear.
Most fear to take such a long and dangerous path.

Stow your compass, your sword, and a loaf of rye;
Tighten and shine thine armor.
A good knight battles many challengers along the way.
Who knows what may be pulled out of a stone?

I find comfort in knowing that God dwells in me, and I in Him,
As I ride my white horse through these haunted lands.

And by the Lord's hand, I shall not fail or falter.
Even when I'm weak and weary, I shall recall
That God called upon thee, and I said, "Send me!"

And when I stumble and fall, the good shepherd shall raise me up
    from the ground and dust the dirt from my eyes,
For God is like a hot fire on a cold and damp night,
And this journey I take on freely as mine—
Union with the divine, ecstasy I find,

Into a cloud of unknowing where all becomes one.

TRIALS AND TEMPTATIONS (THE PATH OF TRIALS)

THE SHEPHERD'S GUIDANCE

Sitting here, I suffer miserably.
Beware your base desires,
For they'll lead you astray,
And the pleasure will be short-lived.

Why chase the wicked ways
When you could be in union with the righteous Lord?
What happens in the shadows
Should not be brought into the light of day.

I am like a lost lamb, and Christ is my Shepherd.
Every blemish on my soul is like a gale wind,
Blowing me off course.
I risk losing sight of the lighthouse.
Lord, mend my heart and my ways;
Guide me back to your flock.

THE BEARDED SOLDIER'S BODHI TREE

The bearded man sits alone in his still study, a light, dreary rain pattering on the window as children's laughter drifts up from below.
A buzzing fly harasses the man, but he is too drained to swat it away.
Rocking in his chair, blankly he stares at the crackling fire.

Burdened by the mundane of domestic life, he misses his simpler life in the regiment and post in the tropics.
Mustering a soldier's discipline, he stands to attention, draws an umbrella, and steps into the drizzle.
Amongst the songbirds and tulips, a cool rain—his burdens turn to smoke like the cannons at the evening parade,
Like a blow to a candle's flame.
He sits under his bodhi tree,
His mind—still and free.
Nirvana.

Chapter 3

The Darkest Hour (Into the Abyss)

Yet, within this dark valley he found himself in, flickered a light of the divine. His path was that of a mystic warrior. He encountered moments of profound insight, glimpses of a truth that transcended the physical world. These were like unexpected oases in a barren desert, offering fleeting solace and a renewed sense of direction. He wrestled with the "mystery of being," sensing a divine presence that eluded easy definition, a treasure hidden within the fabric of space and time.

THE DARKEST HOUR (INTO THE ABYSS)

LOSING MY TEMPER

Swelling,
Swelling up—
      I'm burning hot like a tea kettle.
          Go to sleep, little one!
My blood boils;
    My mind in a vice;
        The stress of today—
           I can't breathe.
              Go to sleep, little one!
                  Father needs his rest.

Crossing the Rubicon, there's no return!
    Rage, rage, rage against this perilous path.

Implosion within.

Emotional collapse.

He's now asleep.
What have I done?

    Regret. Shame. Dishonor.

        You caused those tears to run down that young face.
            What kind of man behaves like this?
                You knew better than to be a monster.

THE DARKEST HOUR (INTO THE ABYSS)

Rest. Give yourself grace. Never again.

Your son needs you. He needs his father to be even-tempered.
You're not a Drill Instructor.
You're a father.

THE DARKEST HOUR (INTO THE ABYSS)

THE BEAST WITHIN

There's a monster that lives inside my home.
I'd like to see him leave.
I often hear him lurking underneath the wooden floorboards,
Scratching beneath my bare feet.
With a creek and a sly peak, he traverses this vessel with ease.
He's always gnawing away at my mind, never giving me the reprieve of time.

This monster likes to move in the shadows.
He'll close the blinds and blow out the candles,
And leave me sitting in the dark, alone with my mind.

This monster likes to stir up chaos.
He'll turn the house into a mess,
And leave me to pick up all the pieces,
And sort this back into neat little lines.

This monster likes the noise of a cling and clash.
He'll pound on some bowls, and cry for hours,
And leave me to cover my ears.

I've sought him out before,
With a spear and shield of mine.
But I could never thrust the tip through.
I guess you could call it a weakness of mine.

THE DARKEST HOUR (INTO THE ABYSS)

I've tried to poison him before,
But the process is never neat,
And I usually get sick before we meet.

For he is like a ghost,
Disappearing for weeks like a fleet at sea,
Only to return to port, forever cruel to me.

I wish to call a priest, to bless away this beast.
With a cross and a wash, God take away this beast,
Of going mad and insane.
I heard the Lord's yoke is light,
For mine is a heavy burden.

It weighs on my soul, making it hard to go forth.
Racing thoughts, bad thoughts, intrusive thoughts.
Thoughts of monsters, they do call to me.
I think I'm going mad.
There's a straight jacket out there with my name.

Please kill this monster,
Or burn the house down.
I cannot bare to live beside,
This wretched beast,
That resides inside my troubled mind.

THE DARKEST HOUR (INTO THE ABYSS)

THE PATH TO CALVARY

Agony in the Garden
The bright moon as witness tonight,
Sand sifts between his sandaled toes,
Praying to Father—
Heavenly tears.
It's the end of the second act; here comes the culmination.
God's will shall be done,
On earth as it is in heaven.

Today he shared bread and wine;
Tomorrow betrayal follows the rooster's crow.
He'll be nailed to a cross on Calvary Hill
Next to a common thief, but not in defeat.

Die as a man,
Rise as a God in three days time.
He'll come again
For the living and the dead,
For thine is the Kingdom, the power, and the glory,
Forever and ever.
Amen.

THE DARKEST HOUR (INTO THE ABYSS)

THE ROSES REQUIEM

Does the rose know what cruel fate awaits?
Today in sunny bloom, the stem long and true,
Its sweet smell gathers a hive of bees.
Many bridesmaids wish to capture thee.

But all that it knows will wither and die.
Tomorrow its petals will lose their colors;
Then piece by piece they'll drop to the earth.
The thorns' piercing teeth will grow soft, and
Its aromatic perfume will linger no more.

The rose scatters to the winds.
Life is short, brutish, and nasty:
Because you are dust, and dust you shall return.

ETERNAL RECURRENCE

One day I'll awake in the divine.
The confusion I'll have in mind.
When I realize this life was just a dream—
Eighty years long, but just a moment in time.

How bittersweet to have returned home
And be reunited with my beloved,
Who has always been with me.

Then I'll return to my life on this eternal day, as if I hadn't missed a beat.
Eventually memory fades,
And I'll want to return.
So I'll lay down in my bed
And drift asleep,
And dream of where I am now.

THE DARKEST HOUR (INTO THE ABYSS)

FROM DARKNESS TO ONENESS

Out of the darkest nights arise the brightest suns—
Moonless, sleepless, restless nights
With distant...
milky stars as company
and frogs holding a midnight quartet.
I could saunter several blocks
without ever seeing another.
Streets illuminated by soft lamps
and the distant murmur of hushed whispers.

As if God had forgotten to shine his tender love on me tonight,
I'm all alone in this somber land;
Depressing thoughts cast long shadows on my soul.

All is near when the birds begin their morning overture
and those first sun rays pierce the horizon—
Like God's army that just landed ashore.
Sweet relief,
I have survived
The dark night of the soul.
Now, divine ecstasy;
Now, union;
Now, oneness;
Now, transcendence with the divine.

THE SEA OF SAGARAM

Life is like a rapid river, composed of three acts.
In the first act, you just let those warm waters rush over you;
Time is barely a concept in your youth.

In the next, you see the sand pass in the hourglass,
So you scramble to collect as many memories as you can,
Sadly knowing you'll forget so many cherished moments,
Like holding your child in your arms.

But in the third act, you surrender to it all
And realize you were the rain, and now the river,
Just making your way back to the sea
Until you decide to become rain once more.

THE DARKEST HOUR (INTO THE ABYSS)

THE FLOWER'S ASCENT

For two hours today the knight fought in the sun.
The battle is over; now he's bloody and weak—
An arrow straight through the spleen.
The brave warrior rests on a stone
And removes his helmet for a final time.
The Valkyries are coming; death is in the air.

He picked up a winsome flower,
So delicate and weak,
Its white petals sparkle in the sun
Like his young daughter's hair.
The knight wished he could see her one last time;
The thoughts of her laughter placed a smile on his face.

He fell back and looked to the sky.
"Lord, take me home."

The flower let loose;
Its petals spread into the air,
Over the field and to the east,
To a little home down the road
Where the meek shall inherit the earth.

Chapter 4

Spiritual Awakening (Transformation)

Along the way, memories surfaced—the vibrant tapestry of his life, both joyful and sorrowful, held within his "shadow box" and of his mind. These memories served as both anchors to his past and signposts for his future, reminding him of what he had loved and lost and what truly mattered. He found moments of connection, fleeting encounters that reminded him of the shared human experience.

THE MYSTERY OF BEING

You won't find God at the end of a telescope,
Nor will you find the divine inside a microscope.
Instead, close your eyes and go within;
Release your ego and take a ride,
Feel the energy swirl inside.

The divine exists in every time and place.
Embrace the mystery of the sages;
Dive headlong into that cosmic bliss.
You're but a drop of rain in the vast sea.

Every flower that ever bloomed,
Every bird that sang a morning song,
Every soul that walked the earth,
Exists there.

Let it dance.
Let it transform your being.
It's all that ever was or will be
In this cosmic dance we call life.

SPIRITUAL AWAKENING (TRANSFORMATION)

WHISPERS OF THE SEA

A gentle soul is like the sea;
Their heart is deep and abounds with life.
They are the poets on the oceanside pier,
Looking out at the horizon during the golden hour,
Immersed in its dreamlike beauty—

An almost unbearable beauty.
God moving over the face of waters,
And the waves crash onto the beach,
Gulls flutter and flap,
The salty spray in the air.

To find mere words to describe it is
An unfathomable task.
For our hearts are so full
That we have no choice
But to whisper it in verse.
This is why we speak so little
But pen so much.

SPIRITUAL AWAKENING (TRANSFORMATION)

THE DANDELION'S FLIGHT

To go deep inside the mind
And break through to the other side,
Like a caver who found Eden in the center of the earth—
To learn this life was all but a dream,
A dream I had dreamt up,
And all I needed to do was to wake up.

To pierce the veil that covers my eyes—
To end the illusion,
To know I'd put myself here,
And everything was going as planned,
And soon I could return back to Eden and vow to never leave again.

This life is but the seeds of a dandelion in the wind
That floats gently by in a blue sky—
A cosmically short event, like a single second in a day,
But yet it was everything—
The big bang itself,
God creating life.

SPIRITUAL AWAKENING (TRANSFORMATION)

DREAM OF EDEN

Where the monarch butterflies dance and play
In a land high in a heavenly sky,
I fell asleep in the Garden of Eden.

I saw a white swan that swam with her cygnets
Through an enchanted pond dotted with lily pads
Where the monarch butterflies dance and play.

As if this entire world were a watercolor
Painted in the mind of God,
I fell asleep in the Garden of Eden.

There, tall oaks twist and turn and hold up pots,
And lilacs sprang like weeds through meadows wide
Where the monarch butterflies dance and play.

And I looked to the sky and saw both silky pink and cool blue
With white clouds floating by on a warm southerly wind.
I fell asleep in the Garden of Eden.

And I awoke from slumber feeling surreal
And looked out my bedroom window to a field of wildflowers
Where the monarch butterflies dance and play.
I fell asleep in the Garden of Eden.

SPIRITUAL AWAKENING (TRANSFORMATION)

LOVE'S LAST ACT

In a moment in the fabric of time,
Forty years since they made their vows—
Through sickness and health, until death do them part—
I saw an elderly couple resting on a hospital bench,
Comforting each other,
Knowing that God was calling her home soon, they sat together, coming to terms—
A day filled with tears,
An entire life together,
The final chapter.

But the encounter reminds me to savor the life I've been given,
For we never know how much time we have left on stage;
The curtains will fall at the end of the play;
We're all just actors playing our parts
In an always unfolding story.

SPIRITUAL AWAKENING (TRANSFORMATION)

MY FRIEND THE GREEN BIRD

I have lived a challenging life lately,
Always longing for the divine but feeling lost inside,
Until one day I saw a green bird in flight,
And I instantly remembered this feathered creature—
And we had always been together.
This bird is my dearest friend;
It stirred my heart and soul unlike anything before.
My dark night of the soul became a bright beacon in the night;
I now knew that everything was going to be alright—
That bird has always been flying by my side,
And one day when the sun sets on me,
I'll follow that bird back home.

SPIRITUAL AWAKENING (TRANSFORMATION)

THE NIGHT OF THE VISION

I heard a whisper one night;
Was I awake or asleep?
I sat up straight and observed
A warm presence in the corner—
A radiant white light being stands before.

"Do not be afraid, my child,"
Stated the figure in white robes.
"I am the divine you seek;
Rest and know that I have heard your prayers.
Fear not, for I have always been by your side.
I am Christ."

I blink, and he's gone;
Lay my head on feathered sheets;
Great peace proceeds;
I return to my sleep,
Never fully knowing if it was a dream or not;
But never doubting that it was real.

SPIRITUAL AWAKENING (TRANSFORMATION)

THE CELESTIAL CANVAS

There is an ember that burns in my being.
It whispers to my soul, let go and transform.
I shall be like an astronaut leaving the earth for the heavens.
To explore the magnificent crimson colors of the universe.
Like clockwork, I am set to launch soon.
I shall paint my mosaic in the stars.

SPIRITUAL AWAKENING (TRANSFORMATION)

A DIVINE TREASURE

There is a treasure I'm meant to find;
It transcends this reality.
There is no map or compass to guide my way,
Just a silent knowing.

Occasionally—
I'll get a glance as we continue
Our distant cosmic dance.

Like warm grass from a recently bedded deer,
I often know when it's near—

This ghostly being
Of the divine kind,
Looking at me patiently
In the eye,

Staring out into the abyss,
Whispering for me to follow thee,
Cleverly guiding me to what I seek.

For what I seek is seeking me.

THE SHADOWBOX

The mind cannot forget what the eyes have seen,
Stored in a photobook within the soul.
Oh, the things that I have seen!

War ships sailing through warm Pacific waters;
I've seen the Buddha glitter in the dark near Pattaya Beach;
And camels lying under palms in crescent lands;
Frosty pines and frozen rivers in Hanguk;
Tiny islands where red blood turned into black sands;
The neon lights of Angels illuminating devils—

A lifetime of memories stitched into the fabric of tiny ribbons,
Daunting challenges held together by a polished badge,
All those fleeting moments captured in time
In a decorated shadowbox on the mantel.

SPIRITUAL AWAKENING (TRANSFORMATION)

BENEATH THE SOUTHERN CROSS

I dream of the day that I can return to the sea—
To captain an old sailing sloop
And sail to the South Pacific's shores
Where my heart was left behind
During a long military float.

The gulls and the whales will keep me company;
I'll dance with the flying fish at dawn's light
And visit the court of King Neptune's might.

A sailor's life is what I'm made for;
My soul belongs to the open seas;
Land holds no place for me.

And if I navigate the stars just right, I'll find myself at home.

Chapter 5

Return and Integration (The Return)

Ultimately, his quest was an internal one. He learned that true strength lay not only in outward valor but in the courage to face his own demons. This journey was not about conquering external enemies like in past campaigns but about confronting the shadows within himself. It was a quest for inner peace, for understanding, for a connection to the divine. And though the path was often melancholic, it was also a path of profound self-discovery, a testament to the enduring strength of a soul seeking light in the heart of darkness.

RETURN AND INTEGRATION (THE RETURN)

BEDTIME LOVE

What a tender moment of love
To tuck my son Oliver into bed.
His golden locks cascade on the pillow like sunlight on a soft cloud;
I brush the hair from his eyes and softly sing sweet lullabies.
We reminisced about his day—
A silly story about a frog he saw in the rain.
We talk about our favorite animals and superheroes;
I cover him under a warm, heavy blanket;
Ocean waves crash on the sound machine;
I stare into his innocent face and smile.

As I leave, he warms my heart and softly whispers, "I love you, Daddy."
And during these dark nights of the soul,
It gives me strength to carry on.
I felt the most innocent of love tonight
In the bedroom of my son.

GREYSON

Little red hairs flow through the air;
He pitter-patters his tiny feet outside my windows' gaze,
Filling the air with his joyful laughter.
He takes me away from the grind of the day
And pauses my work without delay.

A halo of warm sunlight glows behind him,
As if he were a gift sent from heaven.
With a smile, he approaches the window frame
And delightfully greets the lazy cat lying in the warm sun—
A pure moment in time.
For in this moment I knew
That I truly was a father to him,
My wondrous little man.

RETURN AND INTEGRATION (THE RETURN)

A FLEETING JOY

A fleeting joy
To watch my boys swing
Knowing their youth
Will be over in a flash.

And one day,
I won't be able to push them again.
On the old swing set in the backyard.

Time is like trying to catch sand in a net.
Eventually we'll lose the net,
And be buried in the sand.

Today is just a fleeting moment in time.
Like the tear rolling from my eye.

CARRYING THE TORCH

When you're old and gray
And little sand in the hourglass remains,
You'll look back on today
And remember—these were the golden days.

You'll take down those dusty pictures from the mantel,
Staring at you from a time when
Your children could barely walk or stand,
When you were young, strong, and optimistic,
And you'd give anything to go back,
Even if it's just for one day!

So, even though today the kitchen's a mess
And the stress of fatherhood weighs down on your chest,
And some days you want to quit and give up,
Remember, all these days
And all the pain that came with them
Were never in vain.

Eventually, death will call upon you,
But the torch your ancestors lit
And your parents painstakingly kept up
And you carried on
And passed on to your sons
Will continue to shine bright.
For each generation is a torchbearer of its name,

RETURN AND INTEGRATION (THE RETURN)

Keeping the family's cauldron lit—
A light that shines through the confines of time.

RETURN AND INTEGRATION (THE RETURN)

TO THE ROAD AND BACK

This paradox I live with:
When I'm at home, I miss the road,
And when I'm on the road, I miss my home.

When I'm hours away on an overnight stay,
I fondly ponder my loving family—
My two sweet boys with their joyful laughter.
And my loving wife who hopes I'm safe and wonders when I'll return home again.

My home rests on a road where neighbors are like family.
In the backyard, tall grass and wildflowers dance in the breeze below the birdhouse;
My wife's vegetable garden is her Eden of peace among the difficulties of motherhood;
And the boys' sandbox and swings lay ready for play, adjacent to a mud kitchen and little stream.

And yet I know that sometimes I must go;
Adventure awaits the wandering soul;
No good sailor stays in port;
They belong on the open seas among the gulls and leviathans of the deep.
But home is the lighthouse that guides you through your passage;
Even Odysseus returned to Penelope after twenty years away.

RETURN AND INTEGRATION (THE RETURN)

And herein lies the lesson: neither the road nor my home would be as great without the other,
For distance makes the heart grow fonder,
And both places enrich my life.

THE SYCAMORE'S LEGACY

Proudly stood the stately sycamore tree.
The kingly tree of the eastern Savannah.
Adorned with knightly clusters of samaras on velvety green leaves.
It's heir apparent.
In a whirlwind, a mosaic of seeds flies through the sky.
Across the canyons and harbors they sail high above the earth.
Dancing like little embers from a fire.
Over the summits and through the morning twilight.
They are on a voyage far and wide.
Once ready they burrow into the earth
And sprout new life to a new world.

Tiny green seedlings stretching for the heavens.
Delicate and vulnerable.
Nurtured by the forest's deep embrace.
Burgeoning by the seasons.
Until the blessed day.
Coronation.
The flow of existence.

RETURN AND INTEGRATION (THE RETURN)

FRONTIER SACRIFICE: A FATHER'S LOVE

An autumn day on the homestead:
Two young children play in the meadow,
Mother prepares dinner inside,
Father sits on the wrapped-around porch.

A bloodcurdling scream!
Grizzly appears on the tree line!
Mother panics!
Father grabs his rifle
And sprints to the barn.
Now on horseback,
He charges headfirst like a Dakotan brave—

At full gallop, for one last ride.
Children run to save their lives.
Shots ring out, the battles on.
Father and bear melee—
All hung in that savage fray.

Children are safe.
The bear—bloodied and wounded—
Father whispers one last prayer.

A life for a life—
His life for his family.
No higher purpose than to defend his kin today.

THE MODERN KNIGHT

What is a knight today?
Long since swords were pulled from King Arthur's stone,
Long since chivalry lay dead on old castle bones,
Long since the dragons flew the pink skies and inhabited the caves by the sea.

But alas, the knight has existed in every time and place—
Always the peaceful warrior of great virtues,
Always ready for the next gauntlet to fall,
Always ready for the next good fight,
Always ready to bend a knee to God.

Today they may be found battling despots in cold Ukrainian marshes—their hands bloody and cleaved.
Today they may be found raising a family on a homestead—their hands soft like a young child's hand they hold.
Today they may be found caring for the old and sick—their hands tremble with grief.
It matters not the coat of arms that lies on their chest, nor the flag he salutes, or the weapon they holster on their hip.

But if they aspire to lift the bull like Milo,
To play chess like Ruy Lopez,
And their soul is in union with the divine,
Like the yogis of old times,
Then they may count themselves among the knights
Of the modern age.

RETURN AND INTEGRATION (THE RETURN)

THE BEAUTY OF WANDERING

Not all who wander are lost.
I have journeyed for years in search of the ultimate beauty;
My soul cannot stay still.
Some have meditated beneath the bodhi tree;
Others have taken up the cross on the hill.
I've known melancholic seekers who walk miles at night, suspended between the beauty of the moon and the pain in their heart.
The only way to obtain this is to wander away
And to ignore those critics who tell you to stay and that it's all in vain.

A FLOWER RESTING IN HER HAIR

Around the bend of the hospital
I see an elderly couple quietly cry.
One pushes their dying love to their next appointment, standing in line;
All these decades together
Unravel like the bow on their old wedding cake.
Here comes the bride, marching to the sound of organ pipes,
Standing at the altar, a flower rests in her hair.
But what was given by God must be returned,
No matter how used or worn.
Now as organs fail, a long walk to St. Peter's gate;
In three weeks' time, all will be dressed in black—
A lifetime interwoven as one.
Twenty-one guns billow in the morning air;
They'll be together again on the other side of heaven's gate,
But first, a day of dark requiem must pass;
That flower is still resting in her hair.

RETURN AND INTEGRATION (THE RETURN)

ARISE, THE BALLAD OF THE LAST KNIGHT

Arise

Arise

Arise a knight

Arise a knight for thy final act

One last charge to end the age;
The enemy is at the gate;
Raise thy sword and shield and banner bright;
Saddle and bridle and mount the white horse;
Wipe the dust from thy bow.

One last rite—anointing of the sick;
Dread not the pale horseman, but let loose thy courage like the archers' arrows
And meet thy fate boldly,
For after the battle, before the hot fire, let the living find thy corpse with a wicked smile upon its face.

Let them say, a knight has fallen;
Let them say, a good man rests here;
Let them say, arise—a knight.

RETURN AND INTEGRATION (THE RETURN)

BEYOND THE VEIL

One day I hope to close my eyes
And quench my thirst
And look so far into the abyss
That I pierce the veil of reality
And see what lies beyond.

This can't be all there is;
I must wash my eyes;
I must see what really is;
I must wake up from this dream—

The place where all the spirits live,
The place the great faiths call home,
The place we came from—and return.

Some say it's a kingdom, with God on a throne;
Others say it's a pure land where we become Buddhas;
Some—complete emptiness;
Others—paradise;
Some—nothingness.

I think you go wherever your heart lies.
May my heart be pure, so I can see it all.

RETURN AND INTEGRATION (THE RETURN)

THE OLD MAN'S PARADISE

The angel of death delivered the man from a hospice bed;
He departed the world alone and lame.
He was the last of his beloved family to pass,
And he withered away in sadness at an old person's home.

But the next morning he awoke in a bungalow surrounded by palms and orchids;
With waves crashing onto the beach, all his earthly troubles faded into the winds.
There were his dearly departed, happy again,
And he spent his entirety surfing the warm red sea,
Always a hint of salt in the air and a smile on his face.

Now he was home.

www.ingramcontent.com/pod-product-compliance
Lightning Source LLC
Chambersburg PA
CBHW060421050426
42449CB00009B/2075